BE THAT TEACHER

Reigniting the Passion for Teaching and Learning

Felicia
Nicole

Printed in the United States of America by
T&J Publishers (Atlanta, GA.)
www.TandJPublishers.com

Cover Design by Jarvis Releford
(www.BrandNewConsultingGroup.com)
Book Format/Layout by Timothy Flemming, Jr.

ISBN: 978-0-578-66895-6

To contact author, go to:

Website: www.FeliciaNicole.net
Facebook: Author Felicia Nicole
Instagram: FeliciaNicole2020
LinkedIn: Felicia Hill

The dedication of my first published book goes to my mother, Tammy Grubbs Days, the female version of James Evans Sr. from the show Good Times.

Learning begins at home first. Although you are a hardworking woman of few words, your actions taught me a lot about life.

I Love you always and forever.

Table Of Contents

Intro: Be That Teacher

B EING "THAT" TEACHER MEANS SO MUCH MORE THAN lesson planning, collaborating, and teaching the curriculum to students. It takes strength, passion, patience, and constant reflection. It takes having the will to get out of your way, so you have an unobstructed view and understanding of the bigger picture. It means going above and beyond expectations to meet the needs of the students you teach.

The day I walked into my first classroom, I knew what it would take to Be That Teacher, or at least I thought I did. I soon realized that it takes so much more. During my first year, it took self-discipline, meeting with my mentor daily, being a follower and a leader, and being able to adapt to change at the drop of a dime. I had to accept constant feedback and make adjustments. I understood what accountability meant. I rose to the challenge and met the expectations of my administrator.

To Be That Teacher, understand that the students we serve are only as successful as the individuals teaching them. Being that teacher requires that you take ownership of your professional development. It requires interminable days, early mornings, giving up your lunch to a hungry child, going to student games, providing school supplies, smiling, dressing professionally, reporting to work on time, strategically scheduling your time off, and doing what is right when nobody's looking. It requires maintaining a positive mindset, and knowing you can only control what takes place within your building and classroom. Understanding how to relate the content knowledge to who I was as a person helped me to Become That Teacher.

This book will help to improve your performance as an educational professional. Through open discussion and your willingness to reflect on your practices, I hope to spark a mindset shift that will enable educators to push through the challenges they are facing in the profession. Teaching is my passion. I have the ability to coach adults in a manner that is constructive while keeping it real. I've dedicated my life to this work.

I've got a message for you:

If you are in this field because you genuinely want to be a part of the lives and progress of our youth, you need to keep reading to rediscover who you are and BE THAT TEACHER.

BE THAT TEACHER

1: Be A Reflective Practitioner

> *Sometimes you have to sit down with a mirror and reflect on your day, experiences, and the teacher(s) that inspired you the most.*

"I can't do this. I have shown my students how to do it. I have given them one problem, and they do absolutely nothing. They just sit there. They don't even care."

"You all might as well get used to it. I'm not writing any lesson plans. We don't get feedback on them, anyway."

"I just don't know how to reach them."

"After that conference, I see exactly why she acts the way she does in my classroom. The apple doesn't fall far from the tree."

"I'm getting too old for this. I can go home. This year just might be my last, if nothing changes."

Haven't we heard them all before - the frustrations of teachers? My first response to most of their comments is usually nothing but a smile. I give them their time to vent and get it all out. Then I ask, "How well do you know your students?"

My Reflection

As an adolescent girl, I can remember the first time my dad asked me what I wanted to be when I grow up. The first time I answered, I said I want to be a teacher. Over the years, as I grew up, I decided that well, maybe I'll try physical therapy or nursing, but eventually, my heart led me back to becoming a teacher. It was because of teachers like Dr. Sweetenburg, Ms. Brown, and Ms. Lacey that I became an educator. I wanted to be just like them. I wanted to be the teacher that was firm and had high expectations for all students. They were all influential teachers who I aspired to model after. You could tell they took pride in teaching because they came prepared, extremely organized, professionally dressed, and firm. They were the perfect set of role models for a middle school girl growing up on the east side of Savannah. As an educator, I often reflect on the time I spent in middle school. Those were the toughest years of my life, but it didn't seem so bad when you were in their classes.

The first day I walked into a classroom, I became my former middle school teacher. I came prepared. I was excited, and that excitement came out through the delivery of the instruction. I looked like a professional. I was firm and fair, as not to confuse the students. I maintained a level of seriousness for the work I was responsible for, set lofty standards for all students, and I presented myself in a way that enabled me to share my story, without becoming too friendly. Because of my middle school teachers, I knew how to Be That Teacher that reflects daily. Every day I took the time to reflect on my life as a student and determine what affected me the most. Through reflection, I knew that I needed to look the part, mean what I say, and treat all of my students the same way.

Here is a list of suggestions to assist with becoming a reflective practitioner:

- Make time for daily reflection (on the ride home from work, meeting with a trusted colleague or friend, or journal writing before bedtime).

- Be honest with yourself about your work ethic and how it contributes to your performance as a teacher.
- Ask your students and colleagues for feedback without being so quick to respond to it.
- Think about the teacher(s) that left a lasting impression on your life. How do you want your students to remember you?
- Make minor changes after identifying areas of weakness.
- Know that through reflection, we learn.

2: Build Authentic Relationships

Until you put in the time and effort to share your story and listen to theirs, students will be less engaged during the learning process.

Set the Tone

YOU SAY TEACHING IS YOUR PASSION. I WILL ASSUME that you like children and that you like working with them. I'm sure you even stated how much you love them in your interview. However, three months into the school year, you still haven't learned all of your students' names. Before you can get any student motivated in the classroom, build an authentic relationship with them. Be real and be yourself.

Set the tone in your classroom on day one. As students enter your room, they must know that your class is your home, and they will respect it. Students must also feel that they are welcome in

15

your classroom every day. Spend the first twenty-five days of the school year, ensuring that students know and understand the school-wide expectations and expectations for your class. Remember, you are working with children; they need and want structure, just like adults do.

Share Your Story
and Listen to Theirs

Sharing who you are with students helps to develop the climate in your classroom. Listen to your students and learn more about who they are in their lives outside of the school. As a teacher, when you develop meaningful relationships through storytelling, students are apt to listening to you, taking direction from you, and seeking help from you.

Allow your students to share their stories, and you share yours. Take what you've learned about them and determine what connection you have with each child individually and start building a relationship from there. It is an honor to let students know that I came from many of the same circumstances they are experiencing while communicating that we will not allow the world around us to determine who we become.

You won't learn everything about every student on day one. It is a process, and it takes time. It also takes planning. For example, plan a lesson and pull relatable resources. Through modeling and observation, strategically share a little about yourself, family, and friends in a manner that doesn't allow you to deviate from the work and lose instructional time.

Give Private Redirection and Public Praise

Everyone loves to receive praise in public, but not every student enjoys redirection in the same manner. If you can have an open classroom environment that is free and welcoming for mistakes, then sometimes it will be okay for you to provide redirection to students in front of their peers. That depends on the climate and culture of your classroom. As professionals, we must have the common sense to know that if you are providing redirection to the most challenging student in your class and you know he or she does not react well to being redirected in front of their peers, do so privately.

Remember Your Mic is Always On

During a faculty meeting, a wise woman stated, "your mic is always on." Be careful of what you say, how you say it, and who you say it to. Children are smarter than you think. They can sense when an adult is genuine or not. Be careful when referencing students in conversations with your colleagues.

Putting out fires with students and parents about what a teacher said about them can be exhausting for an administrator. It is a situation that should be avoided if you remain a professional.

As a classroom teacher and as an assistant principal, one of the biggest complaints that students made to me was that an adult didn't listen to them. No matter what the situation is and whether a child is in the right or the wrong, listen to them. A practice of mine, especially when a student was upset, I would always tell them to cool downtime first before we can have a conversation. I just didn't want them speaking to me with so much anger within. When they were ready to talk, I would listen. When I dealt with student issues, all parties talked to me openly without being interrupted and without being antagonized by someone else. Once heard, they will accept the consequence for their actions or any next steps I have suggested to correct the situation. Everybody wants their voice heard when dealing with conflict. Why silence the voice of our children?

Hook the Parents

You can build the most powerful relationship with students when you create them with the parents. I've always welcomed parents into my classroom. I also used a communication app to keep them abreast of everything that was going on. I would send notes of concern and praise home to parents. I would call parents as often as I needed to, and my administrator at the time charged the staff with submitting a parent contact log that kept a record of contact about the pleasurable things their child was doing.

Developing a relationship with a parent goes beyond communication about the student. Involve parents. Invite them to become a volunteer for the school. Ask them to chaperone a field trip or school event. Realize that sometimes parents do not know how to help their children. Be that teacher that provides resources, supports, and encouragement for students by engaging the parents.

Here is a list of suggestions to assist you with developing meaningful relationships with your students and parents:

- Be yourself.
- Be professional.
- Develop classroom expectations and be consistent.
- Allow your students to have a voice in the classroom.
- Give private redirection and public praise.

- Communicate with parents. Share the good news first! Ask for help with the challenges the student may have.
- Show interest in the lives of your students outside of the classroom.
- Listen to your students without interruption.
- Share your personal story. Know their story, even if they don't tell you.
- Laugh a little.
- Have real-talk moments.

4: High Expectations

> *Students will work for you, when they know you truly care. There is a big difference between telling them and showing them.*

TEACHERS, DID YOU KNOW THAT THE BEHAVIORS AND work habits you model in front of your students shows them whether you genuinely have high expectations for them. Your work ethic tells your administrators whether you genuinely care about servicing children as an educator. It is one thing to stand in front of your classroom and tell students you have high expectations and will not settle for anything less than, but if your work ethic and energy does not match what you expect, they will believe otherwise. Creating an environment of high expectations for students is critical and must be communicated continuously throughout the school year to students and parents.

Once you have set the tone and established a climate of high expectations, bring the energy, model the expectation, and act as a facilitator. Through my experience as a coach for teachers, I observed many teachers who struggle with this. Take a look at the chart below and ask yourself if you are this teacher.

Bring That Energy	❑ Ready, prepared, and on time ❑ Shows enthusiasm when introducing the focus of learning as if it is the best thing since sliced bread ❑ Dresses the part, gets into character, uses props, etc. ❑ Smiles ❑ Walks around and observes the classroom as if you are ripping the runway! (Not sitting at the desk) ❑ Focuses on the positive and redirects students in a positive way
Model the Expectation	❑ Introduced and explains the purpose for learning ❑ Step by step teacher-led guidance ❑ Allows students to ask questions ❑ Listens and make eye contact with students ❑ Responds in a positive/encouraging manner ❑ Check for understanding and provides clarity, when needed

Act as a Facilitator	❏ Walks around and observes the classroom as if you are ripping the runway! (Not sitting at the desk) ❏ Provides individual feedback to students that is driven by the standard being assessed ❏ Provides whole-class clarity when too many students are having the same misconception ❏ Continuously communicates the expectations ❏ Works with small group ❏ Resolves conflict among students and student groups

The energy you give off will determine the effectiveness of the motivation on the students you serve. If you are not this teacher, work on becoming that teacher.

What having high expectations for students look like in action:

- Employ a high level of engagement in the classroom
- Bring the energy when facilitating instruction
- Model the expectation appropriately
- Show samples of shoddy work vs. proficiency
- Teach in a manner that allows you to build rela-

tionships without using gimmicks continuously
- Assess students throughout the learning progression
- Show and explain student data with the students
- Conference and set achievable goals with students
- Use strategies that will build students' self-confidence in the classroom
- Apply real-world situations and scenarios that students can relate to
- Ask open-ended questions that will make students think

5: Remote/ Independent Learning

Covid-19 became a world-wide pandemic, causing students and teachers to make an unprecedented shift to remote/independent learning from their homes.

IF COVID-19 HASN'T TAUGHT EDUCATORS ANYTHING, IT has exposed a lot of their strengths and weaknesses as it relates to the way we teach using various modes for instruction. Teachers and school systems began developing plans for remote learning to ensure students are still receiving the best education possible. People across the world began to share an understanding of what teachers experience in the classroom daily. While the coronavirus continues to cause a world-wide scare, educators everywhere are working to adapt to a new way of teaching.

The pandemic allowed teachers time to reflect. Teachers began to show empathy for their students. One day, I texted a teacher to check on her progress and offer some assistance, if needed. She stated, "I needed this perspective. I have a better understanding of my students. I truly believe this was God teaching me to be patient and forgiving with my students." At that moment, all I could do was smile and scream out, "Yes"! She gets it now. I had the opportunity to speak with academic coaches and administrative leaders to gain insight into how the students and teachers were being held accountable. I talked to another teacher, and she stated she loved being able to work remotely from home and engage with students online. She confessed that classroom management for her was much better after she hit the "mute all" button.

While social distancing has prohibited you from the typical style of teaching, it has also brought to light some of the professional development you will need to be able to make that shift to remote learning, when required. Work on taking baby steps and come back with a bang for the next school year. Most importantly, Covid-19 has allowed us to spend time with our family, get home projects completed, love their neighbors, and reflect on our profession.

Here are some tips to ensure you are prepared, as a teacher for remote learning:

- Learn as much as you can about the online platform(s) you decide to use
- Invest in headset
- Prepare students by incorporating blended-learning into the normal class setting
- Keep assignments short but relevant
- Have several modes for communicating with parents and students (i.e., teacher websites, phone, email, social media, communication apps, mail)
- Check on your students and let them know you are thinking of them
- Provide feedback to students
- Collaborate with colleagues
- Make a schedule to keep yourself on track
- Give your students a break at times!

BE THAT TEACHER

6: Remain A Professional

> *Some of you are thinking, dressing up in a suit or tie is the definition of being a professional. Some may even think the amount of degrees you have defines you as a professional. It's so much more to it!*

WHILE IT MAY SEEM UNFAIR FOR EDUCATORS TO BE held to very high standards, being a professional and adhering to ethical standards comes along with the territory. You committed to being a lifelong learner and instill knowledge into the students you serve. Committing to this profession means that you are required to be a professional. You are serving as a role model, an example for our youth.

A professional takes pride in their craft. A professional works hard to continue learning and building their capacity. It requires you to be open to learning from your colleagues, administrative leaders, and sometimes your students. There will

be days that you won't get it right. A professional reflects, makes an adjustment, and tries again.
Being a professional requires not only looking the
part but playing the role.

Being able to communicate with your peers
and superiors effectively is a characteristic of being
a professional. Use tact and respond respectfully,
even when you do not agree with others. You should
refrain from abusive or derogatory language. It
also means that you have the mental capacity to
remain professional when students, parents, or
other individuals attack you in an unprofessional
manner. You have to be strong enough to remove
yourself from any unhealthy situation politely.

At some point in time in your career, you
received some feedback. You received constructive criticism that you may or may not have agreed
with. You need to be able to accept feedback, reflect
on it, and make adjustments to do better. Being an
educator does not mean that you know everything
and have all of the answers. It does mean that you
are willing to accept when you do not get it right
and see that it is okay. You have the opportunity to
do better the next day.

Here is a list of what professionalism looks like in action:

- Be prepared and on time for work every day.
- Schedule your doctor appointments in advance.
- Dress the part. Remember, you are setting an example for your students. You should not look like them. Male teachers should wear a sports coat, polo short, or a nice button down shirt. Your appearance may be the only time they get to see a man in a tie.
- Flip flops, short skirts, and cleavage is not appropriate teacher wear.
- The only individuals in the building wearing sneakers should be the physical education teachers.
- Accept feedback and respect the leadership
- Communicate effectively
- Clean up your social media accounts. It should not show that you have a lack of respect for yourself.
- When it comes to the work, Get It Done!
- Communicate effectively and respectfully
- Take Pride in Being an Educator

BE THAT TEACHER

7: Take Care Of YOU

> *If you are not taking care of yourself, you won't be of much help to the students you teach.*

TAKING CARE OF YOUR EMOTIONAL AND MENTAL HEALTH is essential if you want to sustain healthy relationships with your colleagues, students, family, and yourself. Not being able to deal with the stresses of being an educator, parent, spouse, and so much more, will cause you to make poor decisions, have a negative mindset, and react when challenges arise.

Recently, I was surprised with a therapeutic massage from one of my colleagues. I gladly accepted the offer, and it was one of the best things I could do for my body. The massage therapist enlightened me on how my body was reacting to stress and educated me on how to take care of myself. While getting the massage, I allowed my mind to take a break from everything. I was at peace, and all I could do was repeat one of my favorite mantras as she massaged the stress was away.

I observe teachers daily. I get to see them from the outside looking in. I get to see some dangerous habits they have, like eating a full course meal for breakfast and lunch and wonder why they don't have any energy in the classroom. I watch them rush into work late and unprepared and take it out on the students when they are asking too many questions or not understanding the learning focus for the day. I have also listened to them talk about the lack of quality time they spend with their children and spouse. Don't be that teacher.

Find a balance between it all. That can be hard at times. I spend most of my time reflecting in the car on the way home from work. Sometimes I sit in my car in the garage and reflect. I do not take work into the home, unless I am sharing positive news. Exercise your mind in healthy ways, such as reading an enjoyable book by your favorite author, writing in a journal, or focusing on one issue at a time. Be That Teacher who takes care of themselves.

Here is a list of suggestions to assist with taking care of You:

- Practice meditation and in-depth breathing exercising
- Plan a spa day and treat yourself to a massage
- Take a minor break from the work
- Read a book that interests you
- Do something for yourself
- Find a friend that you can open up to
- Exercise
- Eat Healthy
- Reflect daily
- Make quality time for your spouse. Do not discuss work!
- Make quality time for your children. Do things that make them happy.

BE THAT TEACHER

8: Becoming That Teacher

YOU WERE PLACED IN THE POSITION OF BECOMING AN educator because it's your calling. It is your purpose. Walk-in it! Know that every day won't be easy, but it gets better. Remember, you can only control what happens inside of the four walls of your classroom.

The students you serve are depending on you to bring it every day in the classroom. Preparation is vital for teaching and learning. You cannot enter a class and make magic happen. Collaborating with your colleagues helps to build the efficiency of the entire school building. Build each other up. Accept direction and redirection. You do not know everything, and that is okay. Being an educator means that you are a lifelong learner. Do not forget about that part.

It is about the work we do to ensure we are equipping our youth for college, the armed forces, entrepreneurship, or the workforce.

BE THAT TEACHER!

Special Acknowledgments

I would like to thank my husband, Jamie, for always being my biggest supporter. I Love you!

To my dad, John Johnson, and my stepfather, Calvin Days: You were the perfect example of hard work. I never saw you two take a sick day. I never saw you fold under the pressures of life. You always supported me when I was right and showed tough love when I was wrong. I appreciate and love you forever!

Thank you to my siblings, family, and close friends for always supporting my vision. I love you guys.

Thank you to all of the administrative leaders that gave me a chance to let my light shine. Thank you for mentoring me into the leader I am today.- Ms. Patricia Ann English (MCSS), Mr. Vinson L. Davis

(DCSS), Mr. Rodney Bullard (DCSS), Mrs. Ericka Washington (SCCPSS), Ms. Bernadette Ball-Oliver (SCCPSS), and Mr. Brian Dotson (SCCPSS).

To all of the teachers, paraprofessionals, custodians, cafeteria workers, counselors, social workers, front office staff, administrators, and instructional leaders that I've gotten to know, share a smile or laugh with- Thank you!

ABOUT THE AUTHOR

Felicia Nicole, a former Assistant Principal, serving as a District Secondary Teacher Specialist, lives in Savannah, Georgia. Felicia Nicole has experience in the education sector as a Classroom Teacher, Data Specialist, and Academic Coach. Throughout each experience, one thing has always remained constant; she has a genuine passion for working alongside teachers to help them reach their full potential. Felicia Nicole understands the challenges that educators face every day in the classroom - and this is why she authored her first book, Be That Teacher.

Felicia has heard the challenges that teachers face, and through her experience, she understands and urges educators to maintain a mentality of strength. Felicia says that she is "That Teacher" because her mindset will not allow her to quit when challenges arise. She wants to spread insight on how those challenges can be conquered. In Be That Teacher, Felicia provides insight on how to overcome adversity in the classroom and to refuse to give up and leave the field of education.

Felicia Nicole

Let's Keep In Touch

Subscribe to **http://felicianicole.net/** for newsletters and updates. I promise I will not flood your mailbox.

Facebook: **Author Felicia Nicole**

Instagram: **FeliciaNicole2020**

LinkedIn: **Felicia Hill**

CPSIA information can be obtained
at www.ICGtesting.com
Printed in the USA
LVHW021403120620
657940LV00017B/2638